TO

FROM

DATE

Jesus Always Inspirational Journal

© 2018 by Sarah Young

Published in Nashville, Tennessee, by Thomas Nelson. Thomas Nelson is a registered trademark of HarperCollins Christian Publishing, Inc.

Unless otherwise noted, Scripture quotations are taken from the Holy Bible, New International Version®, NIV®. Copyright © 1973, 1978, 1984 by Biblica, Inc.® Used by permission of Zondervan. All rights reserved worldwide. www.zondervan.com. The "NIV" and "New International Version" are trademarks registered in the United States Patent and Trademark Office by Biblica, Inc.®

Other Scripture quotations are from the following sources: The Amplified® Bible (AMP). Copyright © 1954, 1958, 1962, 1964, 1965, 1987 by The Lockman Foundation. Used by permission. (www.Lockman.org). The ESV® Bible (The Holy Bible, English Standard Version®) (ESV). Copyright © 2001 by Crossway, a publishing ministry of Good News Publishers. Used by permission. All rights reserved. The Holman Christian Standard Bible® (HCSB). Copyright © 1999, 2000, 2002, 2003, 2009 by Holman Bible Publishers. Used by permission. HCSB® is a federally registered trademark of Holman Bible Publishers. The King James Version (KJV). Public domain. *The Message* (MSG). Copyright © by Eugene H. Peterson 1993, 1994, 1995, 1996, 2000, 2001, 2002. Used by permission of Tyndale House Publishers, Inc. The New American Standard Bible® (NASB). Copyright © 1960, 1962, 1963, 1968, 1971, 1972, 1973, 1975, 1977, 1995 by The Lockman Foundation. Used by permission. (www.Lockman.org). The NET Bible® (NET). Copyright © 1996–2006 by Biblical Studies Press, L.L.C. http://netbible.com. All rights reserved. The New King James Version® (NKJV). © 1982 by Thomas Nelson. Used by permission. All rights reserved. The *Holy Bible*, New Living Translation (NLT). © 1996, 2004, 2007, 2013 by Tyndale House Foundation. Used by permission of Tyndale House Publishers, Inc., Carol Stream, Illinois 60188. All rights reserved.

Any Internet addresses, phone numbers, or company or product information printed in this book are offered as a resource and are not intended in any way to be or to imply an endorsement by Thomas Nelson, nor does Thomas Nelson vouch for the existence, content, or services of these sites, phone numbers, companies, or products beyond the life of this book.

ISBN 978-1-4041-0603-1

Printed in China
18 19 20 21 22 DSC 5 4 3 2 1

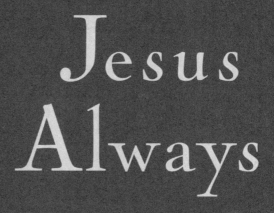

Jesus Always

INSPIRATIONAL
JOURNAL

Sarah Young

THOMAS NELSON
Since 1798

Look for the little pleasures I have strewn alongside your pathway—
sometimes in surprising places—and thank Me for each one.

_____

_____

_____

_____

_____

_____

_____

_____

_____

_____

_____

_____

_____

_____

_____

_____

_____

_____

_____

_____

Rejoice in the Lord always. Again I will say, rejoice!

—PHILIPPIANS 4:4 NKJV

_____ 🌿 _____

I want *you* to share in these blessings, beloved.
Take time, take time with Me.

Shout with joy to God, all the earth! Sing the glory of his name; make his praise glorious! Say to God, "How awesome are your deeds! So great is your power that your enemies cringe before you."

—PSALM 66:1–3

When you are joyful, this changes the way you view the world around you. Even though you see much darkness, you can also see the Light of My Presence continuing to shine.

_____

_____

_____

_____

_____

_____

_____

_____

_____

_____

_____

_____

_____

_____

_____

_____

_____

For I am convinced that neither death nor life, neither angels nor demons, neither the present nor the future, nor any powers, neither height nor depth, nor anything else in all creation, will be able to separate us from the love of God that is in Christ Jesus our Lord.

—ROMANS 8:38–39

_____

_____

_____

_____

_____

_____

_____

_____

_____

_____

_____

_____

_____

_____

_____

_____

_____

The more often you turn your thoughts to Me, the
more you will enjoy My *perfect Peace*.

Whom having not seen you love. Though now you do not see Him,
yet believing, you rejoice with joy inexpressible and full of glory.

—1 PETER 1:8 NKJV

You need to remember that *all the treasures of wisdom and knowledge are hidden in Me.* Remind yourself of this glorious truth frequently, whispering: "Jesus, You are my Treasure. In You I am complete."

————————— ❧ —————————

_____

_____

_____

_____

_____

_____

_____

_____

_____

_____

_____

_____

_____

_____

_____

_____

_____

_____

—————————   ❦   —————————

*He makes me lie down in green pastures, he leads me
beside quiet waters, he restores my soul. He guides me
in paths of righteousness for his name's sake.*

—PSALM 23:2–3

_____

_____

_____

_____

_____

_____

_____

_____

_____

_____

_____

_____

_____

_____

_____

_____

_____

I want you to trust Me enough to cling to Me and follow wherever
I lead, *whenever* I choose. *Your times are in My hands.*

"Have I not commanded you? Be strong and courageous. Do not be terrified; do not be discouraged, for the LORD your God will be with you wherever you go."

—JOSHUA 1:9

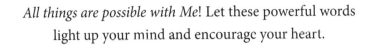

All things are possible with Me! Let these powerful words
light up your mind and encourage your heart.

_____

_____

_____

_____

_____

_____

_____

_____

_____

_____

_____

_____

_____

_____

_____

_____

_____

*For now we see indistinctly, as in a mirror, but then face to face. Now
I know in part, but then I will know fully, as I am fully known.*

—1 CORINTHIANS 13:12 HCSB

_____

_____

_____

_____

_____

_____

_____

_____

_____

_____

_____

_____

_____

_____

My hand has an eternal grip on yours—I will never let go of you!
Moreover, My Spirit helps you keep hanging on.

Why are you so downcast, O my soul? Why so disturbed within me?
Put your hope in God, for I will yet praise him, my Savior and my God.

—PSALM 43:5

Remember that you are royalty in My kingdom, where Glory-Light shines eternally. *Live as a child of Light*, securely robed in radiant righteousness.

_____

_____

_____

_____

_____

_____

_____

_____

_____

_____

_____

_____

_____

_____

_____

_____

_____

_____

Yet I am always with you; you hold me by my right hand. You guide me with your counsel, and afterward you will take me into glory.

—Psalm 73:23–24

_____

_____

_____

_____

_____

_____

_____

_____

_____

_____

_____

_____

—————————— ✿ ——————————

I call you by name and lead you. I know you—I know
every detail about you. You are never a number or statistic
to Me; My involvement in your life is far more personal
and intimate than you can comprehend. So *follow Me*
with a glad heart. . . . I chose to set My *everlasting Love*
upon you. Take time to "hear" Me speaking to you
personally in Scripture, reassuring you of My Love.

You became imitators of us and of the Lord; in spite of severe suffering,
you welcomed the message with the joy given by the Holy Spirit.

—1 Thessalonians 1:6

If you're struggling with a self-centered idea that recurs again and again, try connecting it to a favorite scripture or a brief prayer. This forms a bridge for your attention—away from yourself and toward Me.

——————— ❧ ———————

_____

_____

_____

_____

_____

_____

_____

_____

_____

_____

_____

_____

_____

_____

_____

_____

_____

_____

_____

_____

Fear of man will prove to be a snare, but whoever trusts in the Lord is kept safe.

—Proverbs 29:25

_____

_____

_____

_____

_____

_____

_____

_____

_____

_____

_____

_____

_____

_____

_____

_____

_____

_____

I am the Joy that no one can take away from you. Savor the wonders of this gift, spending ample time in My Presence. Rejoice that this blessing is yours—I am yours—for all eternity!

*Do you not know? Have you not heard? The L*ORD *is the everlasting God, the Creator of the ends of the earth. He will not grow tired or weary, and his understanding no one can fathom. He gives strength to the weary and increases the power of the weak.*

—ISAIAH 40:28–29

Think deeply about *My unfailing Love*. One of the meanings of "unfailing" is *inexhaustible*. No matter how needy you are or how many times you fail Me, My supply of Love for you will never run low.

_____ ⚘ _____

_____
_____
_____
_____
_____
_____
_____
_____
_____
_____
_____
_____
_____
_____
_____
_____

"For I know the plans I have for you," declares the LORD, "plans to prosper you and not to harm you, plans to give you hope and a future."

—JEREMIAH 29:11

I am totally trustworthy, and I reach out to you with *unfailing Love*. I am closer than the very air you are breathing.

So God created man in His own image; in the image of God He created him; male and female He created them. Then God blessed them, and God said to them, "Be fruitful and multiply; fill the earth and subdue it; have dominion over the fish of the sea, over the birds of the air, and over every living thing that moves on the earth."

—GENESIS 1:27–28 NKJV

_____

_____

_____

_____

_____

_____

_____

_____

_____

_____

_____

_____

This joyful journey is all about *perseverance*. As long as
you continue seeking Me, you are on the right path.

_____ ✿ _____

_____

_____

_____

_____

_____

_____

_____

_____

_____

_____

_____

_____

_____

_____

_____

_____

_____

_____

_____

_____

_____

_____

_____

_____

_____

_____

_____

_____

_____

*He who was seated on the throne said, "I am making
everything new!" Then he said, "Write this down,
for these words are trustworthy and true."*

—Revelation 21:5

_____

_____

_____

_____

_____

_____

_____

_____

_____

_____

_____

_____

_____

_____

_____

_____

Whenever you're around someone who irritates you, don't
focus on that person's flaws. Instead, gaze at *Me* through
the eyes of your heart, and those irritants will wash over
you without harming you—or hurting others

For now we see through a glass, darkly; but then face to face: now
I know in part; but then shall I know even as also I am known.

—1 Corinthians 13:12 KJV

_____   _____

_____

_____

_____

_____

_____

_____

_____

_____

_____

_____

_____

_____

_____

_____

_____

When you spend precious moments with Me, I
compensate you generously: I clarify your thinking
and smooth out the circumstances of your life.

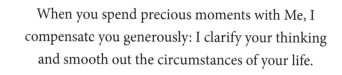

_____

_____

_____

_____

_____

_____

_____

_____

_____

_____

_____

_____

_____

_____

_____

_____

_____

_____

_____

_____

_____

_____

_____

_____

_____

_____

_____

_____

_____

_____

_____

"Do not come any closer," God said. "Take off your sandals,
for the place where you are standing is holy ground."

—Exodus 3:5

_____

_____

_____

_____

_____

_____

_____

_____

_____

_____

_____

_____

Look back over the day, and notice how I helped you navigate your way through it. The more difficulties you encountered, the more help I made available to you. It is good to give voice to My great faithfulness, especially at night, so that you can *lie down and sleep in peace.*

Though the fig tree does not bud and there are no grapes on the vines, though the olive crop fails and the fields produce no food, though there are no sheep in the pen and no cattle in the stalls, yet I will rejoice in the Lord, I will be joyful in God my Savior.

—HABAKKUK 3:17–18

As you become aware of sin in your life, confess it
and receive My forgiveness in full measure.

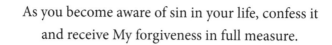

_____

_____

_____

_____

_____

_____

_____

_____

_____

_____

_____

_____

_____

_____

_____

_____

_____

_____

Behold, God is my salvation, I will trust and not be afraid; for the
Lord God is my strength and song, and He has become my salvation.

—Isaiah 12:2 nasb

_____

_____

_____

_____

_____

_____

_____

_____

_____

_____

_____

_____

_____

_____

_____

_____

_____

Break free from faulty self-images so you can view yourself as I
see you—radiant in *My righteousness*, wrapped in luminous Love.

Oh give thanks to the LORD, for he is good, for his steadfast love endures forever! . . . Whoever is wise, let him attend to these things; let them consider the steadfast love of the LORD.

—PSALM 107:1, 43 ESV

Your soul is the most important part of you because it is eternal.

_____

_____

_____

_____

_____

_____

_____

_____

_____

_____

_____

_____

_____

_____

_____

_____

_____

_____

_____

_____

Be joyful in hope, patient in affliction, faithful in prayer.

—ROMANS 12:12

_____

_____

_____

_____

_____

_____

_____

_____

_____

_____

_____

_____

_____

_____

_____

_____

_____

_____

_____

You worship a risen, living Savior! *Blessed are those who have not seen Me and yet have believed.*

He has made everything beautiful in its time. He has also set eternity in the hearts of men; yet they cannot fathom what God has done from beginning to end.

—ECCLESIASTES 3:11

As My cherished follower, you can turn to Me for comfort at all times. Since you have this boundless Source of blessing—*Me*—I want you to be a blessing in the lives of other people.

_____

_____

_____

_____

_____

_____

_____

_____

_____

_____

_____

_____

_____

_____

_____

_____

_____

*For this God is our God for ever and ever; he
will be our guide even to the end.*

—PSALM 48:14

Before you begin a task—large or small—take time
to pray about it. By doing so, you acknowledge your
need for Me and your trust that I will help you.

Let us fix our eyes on Jesus, the author and perfecter of our faith,
who for the joy set before him endured the cross, scorning its
shame, and sat down at the right hand of the throne of God.

—HEBREWS 12:2

In My Presence you can find *fullness of Joy*, *perfect Peace*, and *unfailing Love*. Walk with Me along *the path of Life*—enjoying My company each step of the way.

_____

_____

_____

_____

_____

_____

_____

_____

_____

_____

_____

_____

_____

_____

_____

_____

_____

_____

_____

_____

_____

_____

_____

_____

_____

_____

_____

Don't worry about anything; instead, pray about everything.
Tell God what you need, and thank him for all he has done.

—PHILIPPIANS 4:6 NLT

_____

_____

_____

_____

_____

_____

_____

_____

_____

_____

_____

_____

_____

Don't think of prayer as a chore. Instead, view it as
communicating with the One you adore. *Delight yourself in Me*;
this will draw you irresistibly into communion with Me.

The night is nearly over; the day is almost here. So let us put aside the deeds of darkness and put on the armor of light.

—ROMANS 13:12

_____

_____

_____

_____

_____

_____

_____

_____

_____

_____

_____

_____

_____

One of My names is *Wonderful Counselor.* I understand you far, far better than you understand yourself. So come to *Me* with your problems and insecurities, seeking My counsel.

_____

_____

_____

_____

_____

_____

_____

_____

_____

_____

_____

_____

_____

_____

_____

_____

_____

_____

_____

_____

_____

In the beginning God created the heavens and the earth. Now the earth was formless and empty, darkness was over the surface of the deep, and the Spirit of God was hovering over the waters. And God said, "Let there be light," and there was light.

—Genesis 1:1–3

_____

_____

_____

_____

_____

_____

_____

_____

_____

_____

_____

_____

_____

_____

_____

_____

_____

---

*Morning by morning I awaken you and open your understanding
to My will. I'm always mindful of you, beloved. I never
sleep, so I'm able to watch over you while you're sleeping.
When you wake up in the morning, I am still with you.*

And we, who with unveiled faces all reflect the Lord's glory, are being transformed into his likeness with ever-increasing glory, which comes from the Lord, who is the Spirit.

—2 CORINTHIANS 3:18

A wellspring is a source of abundant supply. Since you belong to Me, My own Life flows through you!

_____

_____

_____

_____

_____

_____

_____

_____

_____

_____

_____

_____

_____

_____

_____

_____

_____

_____

_____

_____

_____

*"I have come into the world as a light, so that no one
who believes in me should stay in darkness."*

—JOHN 12:46

_____

_____

_____

_____

_____

_____

_____

_____

_____

_____

_____

_____

_____

_____

You are no stranger to Me, dear one.
Before I formed you in the womb I knew you.

But you are a chosen generation, a royal priesthood, a holy nation, His own special people, that you may proclaim the praises of Him who called you out of darkness into His marvelous light.

—1 PETER 2:9 NKJV

Seek to spread Joy in the world around you. Let My Light reflect from your demeanor—through your smiles, your laughter, your words. The Holy Spirit will equip you to do this as you give Him space in your life.

_____

_____

_____

_____

_____

_____

_____

_____

_____

_____

_____

_____

_____

_____

_____

_____

_____

Trust in the LORD with all your heart; do not
depend on your own understanding.

—PROVERBS 3:5 NLT

My Love for you is not passive; it actively chases
after you and leaps into your life. Invite Me to open
the eyes of your heart so you can "see" Me blessing
you in myriad ways—both small and great.

Cause me to hear Your lovingkindness in the morning,
for in You do I trust; cause me to know the way in
which I should walk, for I lift up my soul to You.

—PSALM 143:8 NKJV

Sometimes you feel alone and vulnerable—exposed to the "elements" of a fallen world. When you are feeling this way, stop and remind yourself, "Jesus is taking care of me."

_____ ⚘ _____

_____

_____

_____

_____

_____

_____

_____

_____

_____

_____

_____

_____

_____

_____

_____

_____

_____

Yes, though I walk through the [deep, sunless] valley of the shadow of death, I will fear or dread no evil, for You are with me; Your rod [to protect] and Your staff [to guide], they comfort me.

—PSALM 23:4 AMP

_____

_____

_____

_____

_____

_____

_____

_____

_____

_____

_____

_____

_____

_____

_____

_____

_____

Just before I died on the cross, I said, *"It is finished!"* I was announcing the accomplishment of the greatest triumph imaginable: victory over sin and death for everyone who believes in Me.

Jesus said to him, "I am the way, the truth, and the life.
No one comes to the Father except through Me."

—John 14:6 NKJV

_____ 🌿 _____

_____

_____

_____

_____

_____

_____

_____

_____

_____

_____

_____

_____

_____

_____

_____

Many things are simply beyond your comprehension. But do not despair. When you reach the limits of your understanding, trusting Me will carry you onward.

_____

_____

_____

_____

_____

_____

_____

_____

_____

_____

_____

_____

_____

_____

_____

_____

_____

*For by grace you have been saved through faith. And
this is not your own doing; it is the gift of God, not
a result of works, so that no one may boast.*

—Ephesians 2:8–9 esv

_____

_____

_____

_____

_____

_____

_____

_____

_____

_____

_____

_____

_____

_____

_____

_____

_____

_____

Seek to live in the present—with *Me*! Your life is a gift from
Me, consisting of millions upon millions of moments.

"And you will seek Me and find Me, when you search for Me with all your heart."

—JEREMIAH 29:13 NKJV

Do not dwell on the past, beloved. You can learn from the past, but don't let it become your focus.

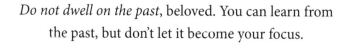

For with you is the fountain of life; in your light we see light.

—Psalm 36:9

As you settle into your rightful position, My redeemed one, your restlessness yields to calmness. This is how I lift you up when you've stumbled.

"For I am the LORD, your God, who takes hold of your right hand and says to you, Do not fear; I will help you."

—ISAIAH 41:13

_____

_____

_____

_____

_____

_____

_____

_____

_____

_____

_____

_____

_____

_____

_____

I want you to cling to Me with tenacious confidence.
This gives you strength to cope with the uncertainties
of living in such a broken, unstable world.

_____

_____

_____

_____

_____

_____

_____

_____

_____

_____

_____

_____

_____

_____

_____

_____

_____

_____

_____

_____

_____

_____

"Therefore do not worry about tomorrow, for tomorrow will worry about itself. Each day has enough trouble of its own."

—MATTHEW 6:34

Because you are a child of the King of kings,
you are capable of so much more than you realize.

"Who of you by worrying can add a single hour to his life? Since you cannot do this very little thing, why do you worry about the rest?"

—LUKE 12:25–26

Even though you wait expectantly, I may not answer your prayers quickly. I am always doing something important in your life—far beyond simply solving your problems.

_____

_____

_____

_____

_____

_____

_____

_____

_____

_____

_____

_____

_____

_____

_____

_____

_____

Therefore, there is now no condemnation for those who are in Christ Jesus, because through Christ Jesus the law of the Spirit of life set me free from the law of sin and death.

—ROMANS 8:1–2

_____

I am the Risen One—your *living God*. Celebrate the
Joy of serving a Savior who is exuberantly alive!

Look to the LORD and his strength; seek his face always.

—PSALM 105:4

Shortly before My crucifixion, I taught My disciples: *"I am the Way, the Truth, and the Life."* I am everything you could possibly need—for this life and the next.

_____

_____

_____

_____

_____

_____

_____

_____

_____

_____

_____

_____

_____

_____

_____

_____

_____

_____

_____

*You will show me the path of life; in Your presence is fullness
of joy; at Your right hand are pleasures forevermore.*

—PSALM 16:11 NKJV

_____

_____

_____

_____

_____

_____

_____

_____

_____

_____

_____

_____

_____

_____

_____

_____

_____

Through My resurrection from the dead, you have *new birth*
into a living hope. My work in you is all about "newness."

When Jesus spoke again to the people, he said, "I am the light of the world. Whoever follows me will never walk in darkness, but will have the light of life."

—John 8:12

Walking in the Light of My Presence blesses you in many ways. Good things are better and bad things are more bearable when you share them with Me.

_____

_____

_____

_____

_____

_____

_____

_____

_____

_____

_____

_____

_____

_____

_____

_____

_____

_____

_____

_____

"Cease striving and know that I am God; I will be exalted
among the nations, I will be exalted in the earth."

—Psalm 46:10 nasb

Joy is the birthright of all who belong to Me.

For the word of God is living and active. Sharper than any double-edged sword, it penetrates even to dividing soul and spirit, joints and marrow; it judges the thoughts and attitudes of the heart.

—HEBREWS 4:12

Align yourself with Me, for *I came into the world to testify to the truth.* Join Me in this quest so that *people living in darkness* can find Me and walk in My *great Light.*

——————— ❧ ———————

_____

_____

_____

_____

_____

_____

_____

_____

_____

_____

_____

_____

On no day will its gates ever be shut, for there will be no night there.

—REVELATION 21:25

Your times are in My hands. My holy hands are absolutely capable of caring for you and meeting your needs.

Jesus answered, "Everyone who drinks this water will be thirsty again, but whoever drinks the water I give him will never thirst. Indeed, the water I give him will become in him a spring of water welling up to eternal life."

—JOHN 4:13–14

_____

_____

_____

_____

_____

_____

_____

_____

_____

_____

_____

_____

Though you may not know the way you should go, you *do* know the One who is *the Way*.

_____

_____

_____

_____

_____

_____

_____

_____

_____

_____

_____

_____

_____

_____

_____

_____

"*When you pass through the waters, I will be with you; and when you pass through the rivers, they will not sweep over you. When you walk through the fire, you will not be burned; the flames will not set you ablaze.*"

—ISAIAH 43:2

_____

_____

_____

_____

_____

_____

_____

_____

_____

_____

_____

_____

Essential preparation for giving a good answer is
living in awareness of My Presence—trusting Me
fully as your Hope. This will steady you as you deal
with the frequent ups and downs of your life.

Do not conform any longer to the pattern of this world, but be transformed by the renewing of your mind. Then you will be able to test and approve what God's will is—his good, pleasing and perfect will.

—ROMANS 12:2

My limitless Love falls continually upon you, like heavenly snowflakes that melt into your upturned face.

_____

_____

_____

_____

_____

_____

_____

_____

_____

_____

_____

_____

_____

_____

_____

_____

_____

_____

_____

_____

*The mind of sinful man is death, but the mind
controlled by the Spirit is life and peace.*

—Romans 8:6

Remember that your adequacy rests in your relationship
with Me. I make you *ready for anything and equal to
anything* by *infusing inner strength into you*!

The Son is the radiance of God's glory and the exact
representation of his being, sustaining all things by his
powerful word. After he had provided purification for sins,
he sat down at the right hand of the Majesty in heaven.

—Hebrews 1:3

When you awaken each morning, say to yourself:
"I am not my own. I belong to Jesus."

_____

_____

_____

_____

_____

_____

_____

_____

_____

_____

_____

_____

_____

_____

_____

_____

*"Whoever believes in the Son has eternal life, but whoever rejects
the Son will not see life, for God's wrath remains on him."*

—JOHN 3:36

The more of Me you have in your life, the more joyful you will be.

"I have told you this so that my joy may be in you and that your joy may be complete."

—JOHN 15:11

Thank Me for the glorious gift of forgiveness. I am your Savior-God, and I alone can give you this blessing.

We love Him because He first loved us.

—1 JOHN 4:19 NKJV

I want *you* to delight in your neediness,
for it is a strong link to My radiant Presence.

The Lord has done great things for us, and we are filled with joy.

—Psalm 126:3

Do not worry about tomorrow! This is a most gracious command.

_____

_____

_____

_____

_____

_____

_____

_____

_____

_____

_____

_____

_____

_____

_____

_____

"I have told you these things, so that in me you may have peace. In this world you will have trouble. But take heart! I have overcome the world."

—JOHN 16:33

I delight in being your Protector,
so you can always find shelter in Me.

"Then you will know the truth, and the truth will set you free."

—JOHN 8:32

The Glory-Light of heaven is perfect and brilliant, without a speck of darkness in it. There will be no sin there—nothing to hide.

_____

_____

_____

_____

_____

_____

_____

_____

_____

_____

_____

_____

_____

_____

_____

_____

_____

_____

_____

_____ _____

Those who look to him are radiant, and their
faces shall never be ashamed.

—PSALM 34:5 ESV

_____

_____

_____

_____

_____

_____

_____

_____

_____

_____

_____

_____

_____

_____

_____

_____

Instead of just thinking about Me, speak out loud;
this gives focus to your thoughts—and to your trust in Me.

The Lord is near to all who call upon Him,
to all who call upon Him in truth.

—Psalm 145:18 NKJV

Invite Me to fill you up to the full with My limitless Love. Ponder *how wide and long and high and deep* is this vast ocean of blessing.

Cast all your anxiety on him because he cares for you.

—1 PETER 5:7

_____

If you're on the verge of sliding into the depths of despair, stop
and declare your trust in Me. Whisper it, speak it, shout it!

You have made known to me the paths of life; you
will fill me with joy in your presence.

—ACTS 2:28

I know about every one of your troubles. *I have collected all your tears and preserved them in My bottle.*

_____

_____

_____

_____

_____

_____

_____

_____

_____

_____

_____

_____

_____

_____

_____

_____

_____

_____

Remember His marvelous works which He has done,
His wonders, and the judgments of His mouth.

—1 Chronicles 16:12 nkjv

_____

_____

_____

_____

_____

_____

_____

_____

_____

_____

_____

_____

_____

_____

_____

_____

Rejoice that I will *still* be with you when you arrive at each coming stage of your journey. Lean hard on My Presence, trusting Me to help you today—and *all the days of your life.*

Beloved, now we are children of God; and it has not yet been revealed what we shall be, but we know that when He is revealed, we shall be like Him, for we shall see Him as He is.

—1 John 3:2 nkjv

I give you these magnificent gifts because *I take pleasure in you.* Let My delight in you soak into the depths of your being—satisfying your soul.

_Yet, O L_ᴏʀᴅ, _you are our Father. We are the clay, you_
are the potter; we are all the work of your hand.

—Isᴀɪᴀʜ 64:8

_____

_____

_____

_____

_____

_____

_____

_____

_____

_____

_____

_____

_____

_____

_____

You may have assumed that your choices are mostly insignificant, but this is not true. A good decision you make today, however small, may set you on a path to accomplish something very important.

These will make war with the Lamb, and the Lamb will overcome them, for He is Lord of lords and King of kings; and those who are with Him are called, chosen, and faithful.

—Revelation 17:14 nkjv

_____

_____

_____

_____

_____

_____

_____

_____

_____

_____

_____

_____

Seek My help with confident anticipation. Be on the lookout
for all the ways I am at work: in you and through you.

——————————— ❧ ———————————

_____

_____

_____

_____

_____

_____

_____

_____

_____

_____

_____

_____

_____

_____

_____

_____

_____

_____

_____

Speaking the truth in love, we will in all things grow
up into him who is the Head, that is, Christ.

—Ephesians 4:15

You are *growing in grace*, but complete freedom from
sin will not be possible as long as you live in this fallen
world. So you need My help continually.

Splendor and majesty are before him; strength
and beauty are in his sanctuary.

—PSALM 96:6 ESV

Come to Me for help, and delight in My infinite sufficiency! *My Power is made perfect in weakness.*

Cast your cares on the LORD and he will sustain
you; he will never let the righteous fall.

—Psalm 55:22

_____

_____

_____

_____

_____

_____

_____

_____

_____

_____

_____

_____

_____

_____

_____

_____

_____

_____

Since the moment you asked Me to be your Savior,
you have had My Spirit living in you. Ask this Holy
Helper to free you from self-centeredness.

If I say, "Surely the darkness will overwhelm me, and the light around me will be night," even the darkness is not dark to You, and the night is as bright as the day. Darkness and light are alike to You.

—Psalm 139:11–12 NASB

I am not a locked barrier but an open door for you—
for all My chosen followers. I came into the world so
that you might *have Life and have it to the full.*

_____

_____

_____

_____

_____

_____

_____

_____

_____

_____

_____

_____

_____

_____

_____

_____

_____

_____

_____

*"The kingdom of heaven is like treasure hidden in a field.
When a man found it, he hid it again, and then in his joy
went and sold all he had and bought that field."*

—MATTHEW 13:44

Let My Love flow through you to others—in both your words and your actions. This *makes My Love in you complete.*

Seek the LORD and His strength; seek His face continually.

—PSALM 105:4 NASB

A much more serious problem is *forsaking your First Love.* If you realize this has happened, repent and run back to Me.

_____

_____

_____

_____

_____

_____

_____

_____

_____

_____

_____

_____

_____

_____

_____

_____

_____

_____

_____

_____

Consider it a sheer gift, friends, when tests and
challenges come at you from all sides.

—JAMES 1:2 MSG

_____

_____

_____

_____

_____

_____

_____

_____

_____

_____

_____

_____

_____

_____

_____

_____

_____

I want you to find pleasure in Me and in My Word. I am the
ever-living Word: *in the beginning* and forevermore.

Jesus said, "My kingdom is not of this world. If it were, my servants would fight to prevent my arrest by the Jews. But now my kingdom is from another place."

—JOHN 18:36

Ponder this glorious truth: I am alive within you! Just as sap flows from a vine through its branches, so My Life flows through you.

_____

_____

_____

_____

_____

_____

_____

_____

_____

_____

_____

_____

_____

_____

_____

_____

_____

_____

_____

_____

_____

"For God so loved the world that He gave His only begotten Son, that whoever believes in Him should not perish but have everlasting life."

—JOHN 3:16 NKJV

_____
_____
_____
_____
_____
_____
_____
_____
_____
_____
_____
_____
_____
_____
_____
_____
_____

Bring Me your *prayers with thanksgiving; present your requests to Me.* Living this way will shield you from anxiety and bless you with *Peace that transcends all understanding.*

*So then, just as you received Christ Jesus as Lord, continue to
live in him, rooted and built up in him, strengthened in the faith
as you were taught, and overflowing with thankfulness.*

—Colossians 2:6–7

I approve of you, My child. Because you are Mine—adopted into My royal family—I see you through eyes of grace.

_____

_____

_____

_____

_____

_____

_____

_____

_____

_____

_____

_____

_____

_____

_____

_____

_____

So we fix our eyes not on what is seen, but on what is unseen.
For what is seen is temporary, but what is unseen is eternal.

—2 Corinthians 4:18

_____

_____

_____

_____

_____

_____

_____

_____

_____

_____

_____

_____

_____

You can get glimpses of My loveliness in the wonders of nature, but these are only tiny, weak reflections of My massive Glory. The best is indeed yet to come— when you will see Me face to Face in heaven.

How priceless is your unfailing love! Both high and low among men find refuge in the shadow of your wings. They feast on the abundance of your house; you give them drink from your river of delights.

—Psalm 36:7–8

Don't fall for the lie that you can't enjoy life until the problem has been resolved. *In the world you have trouble*, but *in Me you may have Peace*—even in the midst of the mess!

_____   ✿   _____

_____

_____

_____

_____

_____

_____

_____

_____

_____

_____

_____

_____

_____

_____

_____

Let us come before His presence with a song of thanksgiving;
let us shout joyfully to Him with songs.

—Psalm 95:2 AMP

If you have *Me*—your Savior, Lord, and Friend—
you have everything that really matters.

And having been set free from sin, you became slaves of righteousness.

—ROMANS 6:18 NKJV

Relax, knowing that you're not meant to be self-sufficient.
I designed you to need Me and depend on Me.

I pray that out of his glorious riches he may strengthen you
with power through his Spirit in your inner being.

—Ephesians 3:16

My Presence will go with you, and I will give you rest.
Wherever you are, wherever you go, I am with you!
This is an astonishing statement, yet it is true.

What, then, shall we say in response to this?
If God is for us, who can be against us?

—ROMANS 8:31

The longer you communicate with Me, the more convinced you'll become of My nearness. *Resist the devil, and he will flee from you. Come close to Me, and I will come close to you.*

─────────────── ⚘ ───────────────

Love is patient, love is kind. It does not envy,
it does not boast, it is not proud.

—1 CORINTHIANS 13:4

_____

_____

_____

_____

_____

_____

_____

_____

_____

_____

_____

_____

_____

_____

_____

_____

_____

The more of Me you have in your life—through
staying close to Me—the more joyful you will be
and the more I can bless others through you.

*As for God, his way is perfect; the word of the L*ORD *is flawless. He is a shield for all who take refuge in him.*

—PSALM 18:30

I am good to those who wait hopefully and expectantly for Me.
Ask Me to open your eyes to see all that I have for you.

_____

_____

_____

_____

_____

_____

_____

_____

_____

_____

_____

_____

_____

_____

_____

_____

_____

_____

_____

*"Be still, and know that I am God; I will be exalted
among the nations, I will be exalted in the earth!"*

—PSALM 46:10 NKJV

_____

_____

_____

_____

_____

_____

_____

_____

_____

_____

_____

_____

_____

_____

_____

_____

Look for and follow the *straight paths* I have for you. I don't promise that these paths will always be easy. But if you walk close to Me, your journey will be much less circuitous.

Therefore, holy brothers, who share in the heavenly calling, fix your thoughts on Jesus, the apostle and high priest whom we confess.

—HEBREWS 3:1

I live in you! I am everything you could possibly need in a Savior-God, and I am alive within you.

_____ _____

_____

_____

_____

_____

_____

_____

_____

_____

_____

_____

_____

_____

_____

_____

_____

_____

_____

_____

_____

_____

_____

_____

_____

_____

_____

_____

_____

_____

_____

_____

_____

_____

_____

_____

_____

_____

"Therefore you now have sorrow; but I will see you again and your heart will rejoice, and your joy no one will take from you."

—JOHN 16:22 NKJV

Your citizenship is in heaven. Someday I will transform
your lowly body so that it will be like My glorious body.

You were taught, with regard to your former way of life, to put off your old self, which is being corrupted by its deceitful desires; to be made new in the attitude of your minds; and to put on the new self, created to be like God in true righteousness and holiness.

—EPHESIANS 4:22–24

Take time to thank Me for the many good things in your life.
I want you to express gratefulness in your prayers, in your
conversations with others, and in your private thoughts.

_____

_____

_____

_____

_____

_____

_____

_____

_____

_____

_____

_____

_____

_____

_____

_____

_____

_____

_____

_____

_____

_____

_____

———————   ———————

Neither height nor depth, nor anything else in all creation, will be able to separate us from the love of God that is in Christ Jesus our Lord.

—Romans 8:39

_____

_____

_____

_____

_____

_____

_____

_____

_____

_____

_____

_____

_____

I created breathtaking beauty in the world, to point
you to the One who made everything. *Without
Me, nothing was made that has been made.*

"For God so loved the world that he gave his one and only Son, that whoever believes in him shall not perish but have eternal life."

—JOHN 3:16

Those who sow in tears will reap with songs of Joy. So do not despise your tears, My child; they are precious to Me.

———————— ❧ ————————

_____

_____

_____

_____

_____

_____

_____

_____

_____

_____

_____

_____

_____

_____

Surely God is my salvation; I will trust and not be afraid. The LORD,
the LORD, is my strength and my song; he has become my salvation.

—ISAIAH 12:2

_____

_____

_____

_____

_____

_____

_____

_____

_____

_____

_____

_____

_____

_____

_____

I have engraved you on My palms because you are eternally
precious to Me. Rejoice in the wonder of knowing that I—the
King of the universe—consider you a priceless treasure!

For thus says the High and Lofty One who inhabits eternity, whose name is Holy: "I dwell in the high and holy place, with him who has a contrite and humble spirit, to revive the spirit of the humble, and to revive the heart of the contrite ones."

—Isaiah 57:15 NKJV

I don't condemn you for your fears, but I do want you to displace them with hope and trust in Me. As you trustingly *put your hope in Me, My unfailing Love rests upon you.*

_____ ❧ _____

And those he predestined, he also called; those he called,
he also justified; those he justified, he also glorified.

—ROMANS 8:30

When you walk in My glorious Light, *My blood continually cleanses you from all sin.* As you seek to live near Me, acknowledging that you're a sinner in need of forgiveness, My holy illumination purifies you.

As the deer pants for streams of water, so my soul pants for you, O God. My soul thirsts for God, for the living God. When can I go and meet with God?

—PSALM 42:1–2

_____ _____